TRAPSHOOTING TECHNIQUES

CLYDE MARTZ

Copyright © 2012 Clyde Martz

All rights reserved.

ISBN:1481164627
ISBN-13:9781481164627

DEDICATION

This book is dedicated to my wife Sue who has encouraged me to pursue my trapshooting hobby ----probably to keep me out of her hair! However, without her support and editing assistance, this project could not have been possible.

CONTENTS

	Introduction	i
1	Selecting Your Gun	1
2	Selecting Your Choke	4
3	Gun Fit and Adjusting Your Gun	7
4	Flinching and the Release Trigger	13
5	Ammunition and Reloading	16
6	Stance	18
7	Where to Hold the Gun	20
8	Movement to the Bird	23
9	Bird Bead Relationship	28
10	Concentration	30
11	Shooting Handicap	32
12	Putting it All Together	34
	About the Author	37

SELECTING YOUR GUN

INTRODUCTION

This book is written to share some insights in the sport of trapshooting that have come from studying and participating in the sport over the last 20 years. The author has been dedicated to the sport during this time and has studied, read, and viewed many things that have been written or produced on the subject.

He has tried many of the things that people have suggested, and as a result, he has formulated some definite ideas of what to do and what not to do - <u>relative to himself.</u> The author knows that an individual's skill in this sport is many times unique to that individual. What works for one person may not work for another.

However, that aside, progress made by any person in any endeavor needs a starting point from which to measure his/her own success. Sometimes that starting point comes from a person who has experienced some degree of success and failure or at worse from a person who has little actual knowledge about the subject.

What the author tries to do here is to share his experience that was successful for him. He hopes you try some of his techniques as a starting point and then measure your own success.

1 SELECTING YOUR GUN

Selecting and purchasing your trap gun is a very personal experience, especially if it is your first one.... I have purchased 21 different trap guns over the last 20 years: 7 Brownings, 3 Ljutics, 4 Perazzis, 4 Berettas, 1 Remington, 1 Kreighoff, and my latest, a Caesar Guerini combo. I don't collect them. I just buy them and trade them off. This is not the way to go! ... I only mention this to show how one can get caught up in pursuing that perfect gun. There is no such thing! Get a good gun, stick with it, and learn how to shoot it! ... Of course, when you fall out of love with it, move on to the next one! If I didn't say that, you would do it anyway, right?

A few factors in selecting your gun:

1. <u>You must like it!</u> ...If it isn't good looking to you and you are not proud of it, you will eventually find a way to get rid of it. The trick is to find a beautiful gun that either fits you, or you know can be made to fit you. You just absolutely know it will break birds!...Good luck....You must first believe!

2. **Almost everything should be adjustable.** If at all possible get an adjustable comb, stock, and rib. You will need that if you really want to progress in your gun fitting and optimize your shooting..... There are many good guns out there that have nothing adjustable. The trick is to find one that fits you and shoots where you think it should. You should try it first. If you can't shoot it to see if you can hit birds, your best bet is to buy something that you can adjust to make it hit the bird... Almost any gun can be made to fit you if everything is adjustable.

3. **Make sure it fits you or can be made to fit you!** (A detailed discussion in how to do this is presented in Fitting and Adjusting Your Gun section.)

4. **Single Barrel or Over and Under?** This is another personal choice. The single barrel gun normally swings better to the bird, but it is tough to shoot doubles with it!... I prefer two guns, one for singles and another for doubles. Today this is approximated with a combo set.

5. **Fixed Choke or Choke Tubes?** Although I am a strong proponent of a full choke for both singles and handicap, I would recommend the purchase of a choke tube gun. This is because it gives you another degree of flexibility in your shooting experimentation

.....It solves that age old question of, "I wonder what would have happened if I had a modified or an improved modified choke in the gun?" ...Of course the answer is.... nothing. After you learn how to shoot well, you will realize that you will hit more birds with a full choke than you will with any open choke in the long run... More will be said about this the Choke Selection section.

6. <u>Remember, there is no perfect gun</u>! There is only the gun you buy, and then you make it work for you... Therefore, buy one that you can adjust to make it work for you.

<u>Have fun in selecting your gun</u>! There is usually no need to rush out and buy the first gun you see... (It is like selecting a good woman/man)! Look at as many as possible and fall in love with your gun!

2 SELECTING YOUR CHOKE

To answer the question, "what choke should one use on singles and handicap" is about as inflammatory a question as one can ask. Obviously, there is no concrete answer to this question. The only consensus is that it should never be anything less than an improved modified (.025). Anything less just has too many holes in the pattern to be a serious contender for top performance... I personally endorse and use a full choke (.035). I use the same choke for both singles and handicap. I want to know that when I shoot the gun, I won't have to worry about any holes in the pattern. If I miss a bird, I know it is because of me and not some stupid pattern holes!

Let us look at the pros and cons of the full choke.

<u>Full Choke – The one that most top shooters use and recommend for both handicap and singles</u>

<u>Pros</u>

- If you are on the bird, you will always hit it. .. This is because there are effectively no holes in the pattern.

SELECTING YOUR CHOKE

- It builds confidence in your shooting since you see excellent results with a direct hit...With an open choke you can be on the bird and may only get a soft hit or no hit at all since the shot is not concentrated. This results in poor confidence for the next shot.......The common wisdom in trap is that you count the birds, not grade them, so don't get caught up with "dust ball" shooting.... Nothing could be further from the truth. If you aren't smoking the bird normally, you are just that much closer to a miss... This is a game of one miss and you are out! So learn to be a precision shooter!

- When a bird gets away from you, you have a higher chance of hitting it because the pattern is tighter.

- It teaches you to be a more accurate shooter. --- (Open choke sloppy shooter, full choke precision shooter.)

- You develop the same process for singles and handicap since you are using the same choke.--- Changing chokes is like changing guns. ... Don't do it unless you think you must.

Cons

- It gives the illusion that the bird is harder to hit, since the pattern is smaller.... However, this is false since more shot is brought in toward the target resulting in a higher density around the target than with an open choke. ... The "dust ball diameter" is actually bigger for a full choke than an open choke since the peripheral shot is now concentrated more around the center.

- There are no others....

3 GUN FIT AND ADJUSTING YOUR GUN

There are several key areas you must optimize to ensure the gun fits you. It must shoot properly and comfortably... These areas are length of pull (proper placement of face on stock relative to the hand), bead alignment (rib and stock height), point of impact (height of shot pattern), and recoil management.

Length of Pull

The length of pull is the distance from the heel of the stock to the trigger, and is very important. Most gun manufacturers make this distance approximately 14 1/2 to 14 3/4 inches, which is too long for 60% of the men and 90% of women and youth.

Here is how to test and set your length of pull.... Shoulder the gun and bring the gun to your face, not your face to the gun. Now note where your thumb is relative to your nose/face. It should be no more than 1 1/2 to 2 inches (maximum) from your front knuckle of the thumb. With this position, it is easy to lock the gun into your face which results in the gun barrel naturally moving to where your eye goes - to the bird. If you have a greater distance between the thumb and nose, the gun is much more difficult to control when you start chasing the bird..... I am not very tall and I use a 13 1/2 inch length of pull! It wasn't until I cut my stock that my gun really moved well and with total control to the bird.... The closer your nose is to the thumb, the more control you will have on the gun movement.

Bead Alignment

Bead alignment is also very important. If your beads aren't aligned properly you will never hit the bird consistently.

To accomplish this is quite simple if you have a gun with an adjustable stock.... If not, there is always sandpaper and a wood file! ....Set your gun so you see a figure 8 with your front and middle beads. With your head buried into the stock, mock up the same pressure you will be using when you are firing the gun. Make sure there is no space between the beads. This is one of the biggest mistakes a beginning shooter makes. The figure 8 is important because it is easy to replicate each time you mount the gun.

If the beads don't make a figure 8, move the stock cheek piece until they do.

Point of Impact

The point of impact is where the center of the shot pattern hits the target relative to where you are aiming. Most data is given at 40yds, i.e. so many inches high at 40yds.... For example if your gun is shooting 15 inches high at 40yds it is said to shoot 100/0 or a pattern high. (A full pattern at 40 yds is about 30 inches in diameter). 12 inches high at 40 yds is 90/10, 9 inches is 80/20, 6 inches high is 70/30, 3 inches high is 60/40, and dead on is said to be 50/50.

To adjust your point of impact is also very easy if you have an adjustable rib gun. If not, don't sweat it since most production guns are set for 60/40 (3 inches high at 40 yards). This is what I shoot now after many years of shooting 90/10. All of this assumes that you are shooting a figure 8 with your front and middle bead. Again, always shoot a figure 8, since that is the basic reference point for every change you make.

Now to adjust your point of impact... If you want your gun to shoot lower, you must lower the front end of your barrel relative to the rib. This means the distance between the barrel and the rib at the front increases. Make sure you still keep a figure 8 in your sight picture. In most adjustable rib guns, there is a mechanism at the front end to allow you to do this....In some guns you may have to adjust your cheek piece to maintain a figure 8.

To raise your point of impact, the reverse of the above needs to be followed... raise the front of the barrel relative to the rib, i.e. decrease the distance between the end of the barrel and the rib.

Some guns like the **BT-99 Plus** allow you to adjust both the front and rear ends of the barrel, giving you absolute total flexibility. Whatever you do, remember to keep the beads at a figure 8. Screw that up and you will have created a lot of grief for yourself.

Since I normally hold a relatively low gun on the trap house and swing through the bird, I set my gun for 60/40 to 50/50 (flat shooting)..... If you hold a higher gun and do not swing through the bird, you may want to set your gun at 70/30 or higher to have the gun do some of the work for you. Many good shooters hold a high gun with good results.... However, it is much easier to make a mistake with a high shooting gun than it is with a low shooting gun when using a swing through the bird style. This is because you must always remember to be under the bird.... A big problem for me at times.

I have had success with both high shooting and relatively flat shooting points of impact. However, I now find it much easier to shoot good scores with a relatively flat shooting gun since I am swinging through the bird and using that motion to clear the bird and provide the necessary lead.... It also seems to "smoke" the bird better.

An easy way to determine your point of impact is to take a target box, mark a circle on it about the size of a silver dollar, set the box 20 yds away (20 big steps for me), lean your gun against a tree (or something stable), hold it steady, cover the circle with your front sight and fire... Then draw a line through the center of your pattern and the circle. Measure the distance and multiply by two. That is how high your gun is shooting relative to 40 yards.... I do this several times a year to know where my gun is really shooting.

Recoil Management

One of the biggest things that allows us to enjoy shooting is the management (reduction) of recoil. This can be done in several ways: reduce the shell charge, add weight, mechanical shock absorbers, or alter the gun to reduce the felt recoil.

- ### Reducing the Shell Charge

    Going from a 1 1/8 to a 1 oz load will obviously reduce the

felt recoil. The lower the shot weight, the lower the recoil...... For example, if you reduce the shot weight by 1/8 ounce , e.g. 1 1/8 to 1 oz. the felt recoil is reduced by 11% (.125/1.125) if everything else is the same. Of course, we all know that when we reduce the shot size, an increase in powder is used most of the time to achieve the equivalent dram effect. Therefore, the felt recoil is not reduced by 11%, but something like 7% - still a significant amount.

However, from a performance point of view, I believe there is no advantage of using a 1 oz load if one can tolerate the recoil from a 1 1/8 oz load. There does seems to be, however, an advantage with the 1 1/8 oz loads in the long run. One miss and you are out of most trap tournaments!...... More shot, more probability of kills!

- **Adding Weight**

The easiest way to reduce recoil is simply add weight to the gun. I put at least 8 - 10 ounces of lead in my stock and that really seems to help. Standard mercury recoil reducers can be purchased to fit in most stocks that require little or no alteration. The heavier the gun the less recoil you will feel. So get the heaviest reducer that can fit in your gun!.... Since the added weight is in your stock next to your shoulder, it affects the gun swing very little.

- **Mechanical Shock Absorbers**

Many shooters use some kind of mechanical device to help absorb (stretch out) the recoil. They are very popular, and I have used a number of them. And I think, in general, they work very well. However, they are expensive and from my experience they are not any better than adding weight and making a few simple alterations to the gun.

- **Altering the Gun**

Two simple alterations to the gun will also significantly reduce the recoil:

1. The first is to make sure you have a long forcing cone...Many new gun makers now know the advantage of long forcing cones and they are now normally standard. Guns such as Beretta, Browning, Caesar Guerini, and others now come with long forcing cones... If you buy a gun with a short forcing cone (less than 1 inch), get a competent gunsmith to lengthen your cone anywhere from 3 to 5 inches. You will notice a big difference in your felt recoil.

2. The second is to have a "fall away comb" on your stock. What I mean is the comb should not be straight, but have a very slight "twist". The comb is slightly twisted clockwise (for a right handed shooter) looking down on the comb. This will make sure that when the gun recoils, it "falls away" from the face and not into the face. Hence, the term a "fall away comb". The opposite is true for the left hander.

4 FLINCHING AND THE RELEASE TRIGGER

I remember the time, about 2 years after I started shooting, I developed a flinch so badly I was afraid I would drive the barrel into the ground! I was just about ready give up when something wonderful happened.

I was at a large tournament in Pennsylvania and was lamenting my problem to a friend of mine during dinner. Across from me was one of Pennsylvania's top shooters who was listening to our discussion. He asked if he could join us and I said that would be fine. He then proceeded to tell me how to correct the problem. As you might guess, he said that I was a strong candidate for a release trigger. He told me how to make that transition, which is the real purpose of this chapter. He said:

- First you make the commitment to get a release and place it in your gun. (This is easier said than done! Many shooters do not have a drop out trigger and for many that decision is difficult to make.) For the avid hunter this seems to be a big change. But it really isn't. This is because flinching usually occurs only in repetitive shooting. Hunting of course is not repetitive shooting. Therefore, most of the time it is easy to hunt

FLINCHING AND THE RELEASE TRIGGER

with a pull trigger and use a release for trapshooting.

- Second you need to learn how to shoot it <u>before you ever fire your first shot on the line.</u> You do this by going to the basement, or some place where no one is around, and dry fire it many times pretending you are shooting at a bird. (I think I did it for 500 times!) He also said too many people think they can just put the release in, go to the line and shoot. Many times that results in failure, because the mind and body have not been conditioned to the release. Repetitive dry firing cures that problem. However, he also said that once you do this, it may be impossible to return to a pull for repetitive shooting...... I have found this to be very true in my case.

Now for the basics of the release trigger. I am very picky about my releases. Here are some of the things that the gunsmith does when he builds a release for me:

1. Makes sure the trigger is very smooth. This is done by polishing the contact surfaces so nothing is rough or grabs.... It is not uncommon, in my case, to have the gunsmith work on my trigger several times.

2. Sets the trigger for a 5 pound pull.... I like a fairly heavy set. Certainly no lighter than 4 pounds... Make sure he uses a good trigger scale.

3. Sets the trigger for a 2 pound release. This means that when he pulls the trigger it sets at 5 pounds and when he lets up on the scale it goes off at 2 pounds... Anything less than a 2 pound let-off is too slow for me.

In summary, if you are having a flinching problem, get yourself a release trigger, make the commitment, and learn how to use it. Your problem should go away. Mine sure did. I have not really flinched since I went to a release more than 20 years ago.

5 AMMUNITION AND RELOADING

The age old questions of what kind of shells are best and should you reload or not is debated all the time.... If you have a big pot of money, you should shoot new premium shells all the time, e.g. AA. STS, Federal Premium. However, for most of us money is limited, and we must shoot a cheaper shell or reload our shells.

I find that if you are careful in your reloading process, you can produce shells that are significantly better than the cheaper brands, and rival the new premium shells. This assumes that you use premium components with hard shot. The cost difference between good reloads and the cheaper shells is very small. So today you reload only because you can produce a better quality shell than the economy shells on the market, not to save money.

In my case I prefer reloads because I take great care in reloading and only use the best components available.... My favorite reload is 1 1/8 oz #8 shot (only West Coast or Lawrence magnum), STS hull (shot no more than 4 times), Claybuster Figure 8 wad, Winchester 209 primer, and 17.3 grains of 700X. I use this load from 16 to 25 yards and the birds just evaporate with my full choke. The only thing I change at 27 yards is to go to 7 1/2 shot. This works very well for me. Try it - you might like it!

As an aside, I also find in the reloading process that extra care needs to be taken so that your reloads are consistent, especially in the powder charge. An uneven charge bar movement which can easily occur in manual loaders can dramatically change your powder charge. For this reason I have gone to the **MEC** electric **(9000E)** and really like the results.... Any automatic smooth charge bar movement machine is better than a manual movement.

6 STANCE

A shooter's stance is determined by how he will most easily deliver the shot in the most difficult direction from the post where he is standing.... For example, a shooter on post 1 should position his feet so that when he raises the gun to the trap house, the natural position will be over the left edge of the house. In this position he should be able to swing either right or far left (the most difficult movement on post 1) with minimum effort.

To determine the foot position, place the gun on the shoulder, point it to the trap house naturally, and take little steps to the right or left until the gun is over the left edge of the trap house. Note where your feet are. This is the natural position for you to stand on post 1.

For post 2 do the same thing by having the gun point half way between the left edge and the center of the house. For post 3 point the gun at the mid point of the trap house. For post 4 halfway between the middle and the right edge and for post 5, the right edge of the house.

In summary, at each post point the gun toward the trap house from a natural position on your shoulder to where you can best swing the gun to any angle that the bird emerges. Observe where your feet are, and this is where you stand.

For the most part your legs should be fairly straight, definitely not bent, with approximately 70% of your weight on the left leg for a right hander, and the opposite for a left hander. The reason for this weight distribution is that it will be much easier to swing the waist in the direction of the bird.... Of course, you can swing your arms from any position. Remember: arm swing is bad; waist swing is good!

Strive to swing your arms as little as possible. Learning to swing at the waist helps keep the gun against the face, helps maintains proper bead alignment, and reduces the probability that you will jerk to the bird. Learning to swing with your waist more than your arms is very important in handicap.... Waist swinging over arm swinging is extremely important in shooting handicap because arm swinging magnifies any errors you develop in your swing.

7 WHERE TO HOLD THE GUN

Where you hold, or point the gun, on the trap house is an another age old question. Many successful shooters hold on the house, or 1/4 way up from the front trap house edge (the edge away from the shooter) to where the bird peaks, or 1/2 way up, or 3/4 way up. So there is no right answer for everyone. ... However, I will explain what I do and you can judge accordingly what you may want to try... I am also a two eye shooter.

<u>My Style - Hold Relatively Low, Usually on the Trap House, but Never More Than 1/4 to Peak of the Bird</u>

I believe it is important that you see the bird as clearly and as quickly as possible... The quicker you see the whole bird, not the flash, the easier it is to begin a smooth swing. Therefore, most of the time I hold relatively low -----on the front edge of the trap house most of the time but never more than approximately 1/4 up to where the bird peaks.... And I only move to this height if the wind is very calm. This allows me to see the bird quickly, more quickly than if I were holding high above the house. It also forces me to develop a smooth swing to the bird..... (The higher you hold, the quicker you can get to the bird, but the probability is also higher that you will jerk your gun to the bird. Jerking the gun is the kiss of death for a long string of hits.).... Then just as I am passing the bead through the bird (clearing the bird), I pull (release in my case) the trigger and let my gun movement develop the necessary lead.

Where to look for the bird is also very important. A few instructors say look at the edge of the house and look hard for the bird to come out. I think that is dead wrong! Looking hard at the edge of the house can cause you to not see the bird at times and at other times cause you to jerk shoot at the bird! ...I look over the gun barrel above the trap house with a soft focus, and lock on to the target as quickly as possible.... Your peripheral vision will help you pick up the target as it comes out of the house.... See the whole target, not the flash. Then begin a smooth but quick movement to the bird. Swing as quickly as you can with the gun under control to the bird, and just as you are passing the bead through the bird, pull/release the trigger. <u>Do not stop the gun</u>. You want the natural gun movement to provide the lead on the bird so the shot string can work and explode the target for you. You will be surprised how hard you will hit the bird with this style! This technique is especially good on windy days......

<u>The technique recommended for the one eye shooter is to hold the bead below the trap house edge at all times.</u>

This is because if you use only one eye, it is easy to have the barrel block the bird if your gun is anywhere above the top of the trap house. ----Seeing the bird as quickly as possible after it leaves the trap house is key to getting quickly and smoothly to the bird!

Holding Above the Trap House Style

Many shooters hold their gun high above the trap house with great success, either in the 1/2 or 3/4 way up to the bird peak. This style is particularly successful when the birds have very little variation, such as on a very calm day. Gun movement to the bird is smaller than when holding near the trap house.

However, when the birds start moving around a little such as on a windy day, this style is not nearly as effective as holding a relatively low gun and driving through the bird. This is because the probability of jerking to the bird is much higher since the swing is shorter and you have a shorter time to make a smooth quick swing to the jumping bird.

If you are holding a low gun, you have a longer time to get to the bird resulting in a smoother swing.

That aside, you should try both styles to see which one you like best in all kinds of conditions..... (The person who can hit all the birds, especially on a windy day, will usually win the tournament. Almost anyone can shoot a good score on a calm day. But when the wind comes up, that is where we separate the shooters.).....I have shot both high and low guns quite successfully. But overall I prefer the low gun style because I see the bird quicker, longer, and better.

8 MOVEMENT TO THE BIRD

Before you begin your movement to shoot the bird, make sure you have the proper stance, proper gun fit, and are pointing the gun correctly toward the trap house. These topics are covered elsewhere in this booklet.

Face and Gun

The first thing you do is bring the gun to your face, not the face to the gun. Place the gun firmly in your hands and to your face, not too tightly but firm enough that you feel in absolute control... When you want to move the gun, the gun must do what you want it to. It must not feel "loosey-goosey". If you need to make a quick move to the target, the gun must respond.

Freeze the Gun Right Before You See the Bird

This means absolutely no movement! Many shooters seem to move the gun right before they see the bird. If the gun is going in a different direction relative to the bird direction as the bird comes out, you must make a correction. This usually means lost time and a higher potential for a "jerk" to the bird with a corresponding lost bird. Jerking the gun a big "no-no". Freeze the gun until you see the bird clearly. Then go smoothly and quickly to the bird - no jerks!

Line up the Beads - Again

Make sure the beads are lined up properly. Many well intended instructors say this is not necessary. They say this has been done in fitting your gun and this should not be necessary here. Baloney! Take every opportunity to make sure the beads are lined up properly in a figure 8..... Remember, this is a bird bead game. That means not only the front bead is relative to the bird, but also the barrel's two beads must be aligned properly. Nothing else matters if the beads are in the wrong place when you shoot at the bird. You just will not hit the bird!

The Call

In today's trap the Call is not as important as it once was

because of the electronic voice pulls. However, the Call is still important to you. A loud call normally means you will aggressively go after the bird. A low level call means you will probably meekly go after the bird. Try to be somewhere in between.

Pressure Between Head and Stock

The cure for lifting your head is a constant pressure between the face and stock throughout the swing....Once you have your face on the stock and you are tightly into the gun, note the pressure on your face.... This pressure must be maintained throughout the swing and through the delivery of the shot! This will usually guarantee two things: one, you will not lift your head, and two, you will deliver a crushing blow to the target if you are lined up properly.

Smooth to the Bird

Remember, when you make the Call and begin your movement to the bird, be careful to eliminate all jerky movements and concentrate on being smooth but quick to the bird. Many people use this as their trigger thought right before they call for the bird. (This is covered more in the Concentration Section of the book). Remember, you must be smooth to the bird!

MOVEMENT TO THE BIRD

Move the Waist, not the Arms

Many of us get into a bad habit of moving our arms instead of our waists when we are going to the bird. When we move the waist we are in much better control of our movement than if we move our arms. This is because the body will reduce most of the jerks to the target because of its larger inertia, whereas the arms are lighter and more prone to jerk to the target. An arm swinger can get away with it on the 16 yard line, but very little success will be found at the long yardage for such a swinger.

That aside, all shooters move their arms! But it should just be kept to a minimum. Try desperately to move the waist as much as possible, instead of the arms.

Shot String and "Clear the Bird"

One of our greatest trap shooters in the game gave me a very important piece of advice. It was so important to me that it is the last thing I think about before I call for the bird.....As most of you know, there is a shot string of 10 to 15 feet flying out at the bird. This means if you shoot right at the bird or near the back end of the bird, you have a high probability of not breaking the bird! But if you place the shot string in front of the bird, it usually turns into a dust ball. The bird literally get ground up by the shot string. This is extremely important! ...(As an experiment sometime, try shooting way in front of the bird at the long yardage, or any yardage, and you may find it very difficult to miss it)... Nothing has increased my performance more than my effort to say to myself "clear the bird dummy" <u>right before</u> I call for the bird.

9 BIRD BEAD RELATIONSHIP

Another very important area in trapshooting is the relationship between the bird and the front gun bead. No one ever broke a bird without the proper relationship between the bird and the bead/barrel... Many good shooters claim they never see the bead when they deliver the shot. They do, except they don't realize it. It is there, if only in a ghost like image. Otherwise they would be just instinctively shooting and praying they hit the bird - which is impossible for a long string of hits.

One of the world's greatest trap shooters told me, "If you don't know where the bead and bird are when you deliver the shot, you might as well take up bowling, cause you will never learn to be consistent at trap shooting".

I believe that all excellent shooters achieve a very good bird bead relationship skill, even if they don't realize it!

Another myth in trap shooting is that "you point the gun to break the target". That may work in quail and pheasant shooting. But in trap shooting it is an utter failure....What you do is like dynamic rifle shooting. You swing the gun smoothly and quickly (no jerks), get the right bird bead relationship very quickly, and then pull (or in my case release) the trigger. If that isn't dynamic rifle shooting, I don't know what is!.... This is how you become successful at hitting bird after bird. In trapshooting, as opposed to hunting, you must hit every bird. That is why "pointing and shooting" does not work.

10 CONCENTRATION

We have often heard the expression in trap, "I lost my concentration and I missed the bird". This is so true many times. But just what is concentration? Very few shooters can explain it.... Concentration is nothing more than what you think about <u>right before you say "pull". It is nothing before that time or after that time.</u> It must be clearly visualized in your mind and nothing should enter your mind except that thought at that moment.... (A very top shooter called it the "trigger thought")....After you deliver the shot, you totally relax and think about anything you want to until you are ready to deliver the next shot.... It is literally impossible to keep a strong concentration thought for a long period of time!

The trick is what to think about right before you say "pull" or what is your "trigger thought"?

You should strongly think about the most important thing you want to execute, i.e. what you need for success. There may be more than one, but pick the most important one to you. The others will fall into place ....For example, in my case I say to myself, "clear the bird dummy", since I know I want the shot string to work for me. I know if I shoot at or behind the bird, I will probably not hit it. I keep that thought right through until

I shoot. ... Another thought my be "bead under bird" (One that I used for years when I was using a high shooting gun). ... Your thought should be whatever your most important image is that gives you success in breaking the bird.... Then make it happen by having it as your last thought!.... <u>Think about it and say it to yourself every time you get ready to call for the bird.</u>...In my case, many times I say it out loud to myself..... If you learn to do this, you are well on your way to hitting a long string of birds by ensuring your mind does not wander from the job at hand. You want your mind to think about the same thing every time you get ready to call for the bird!

Another thing that I hear many times is that, "I started thinking about what I was doing and I began missing birds"....This, more than anything, is a sign of a very amateurish shooter! You must be thinking all the time or you will begin missing birds and not know why. The trick is to think about the right things in a positive way and know how and what to think. I try to explain this in considerable detail in this book.... Always keep thinking and know what you are going to do before you do it! That is the only way you can overcome the pressure when you need to break that last 25 birds for that perfect score!

11 SHOOTING HANDICAP

Shooting handicap targets is almost like shooting singles with the following exceptions:

1. Since the birds are further away, everything is just a little bit slower and more deliberate . For me the hold point on the trap house does not change much. If it changes at all, it is a little bit lower. The reason is that I am trying to set up the shot delivery so that the swing is similar to singles.

2. The most important thing is that you must clear (lead) the bird a little bit more than in singles. This is obvious since the bird is further away from you... If you are using a swing through the bird style, such as when holding a low gun on the trap house, the motion of the gun will usually do this for you and nothing needs to change much... However, if you are holding a high gun, special care must be taken to deliver the shot further from the bird than you do in singles because the gun movement is not working as much for you.

3. As long as I am shooting from the 24 yard line or less, I do not change my load. It is the same as described in the Ammunition and Reloading section of this manual... It is half way between a 2 3/4 and 3 dram load... From 25 to 27 yards, all I change is the shot size - from 8 to 7 1/2.

12 PUTTING IT ALL TOGETHER

I assume you have read everything in this manual and you are now going to the firing line. You have set up your gun, have in the right choke (full, I hope), and you know exactly where the gun shoots with figure 8 beads!

This section is designed to help you do just that, step by step.... Here is what you should do and how you should think.... (The assumption is also made that you are not a first time shooter and you are knowledgeable about trapshooting basics and have incorporated them in your shooting procedures, e.g. safety, dress, shooting etiquette, and ATA rules for the shooting line).

1. <u>Stand behind the line and observe</u> how the birds are flying. If they are not acceptable, try to get them reset.... Don't make a federal case about this especially if everyone has to shoot on the same traps.

PUTTING IT ALL TOGETHER

2. <u>Approach the line with confidence</u> and not fear. (Many shooters fear the first shot and as a result a miss becomes a large probability).... This fear is usually overcome by remembering the concentration process outlined in this book. Think about what it takes to be successful, not what it takes to fail... Never approach the line with a negative attitude. Be serious about hitting that bird and you will hit it!

3. <u>Set your feet in the proper position</u> as outlined in this book and do not move them. Lock them into position.

4. <u>Watch the birds carefully (see them clearly) when the previous shooters fire</u>. This is so you will be ready to see the bird clearly when it is your turn.

5. <u>Be eager to take your turn shooting without fear</u>. ...Believe you can turn that bird into dust!

6. <u>Mount your gun confidently and firmly</u>. See the figure 8 of the beads, feel the pressure on your face from the stock, and then feel the same pressure as you shoot and after the shot. Let the gun know, and everyone else around you, that you are in charge!

7. <u>Relax now and point the gun near the front edge of the trap house</u>, or whatever height you want to point the gun.

8. <u>Look above the barrel and trap house eagerly with a soft focus</u> and be ready to see the bird clearly right after it comes

PUTTING IT ALL TOGETHER

out.

9. <u>Now is the time to concentrate.</u> ... Think about that one major_thing, (your "trigger thought") that will give you success, e.g. "bead under bird", or "smooth to the bird", or as in my case "clear the bird". This is very important. <u>You do this every single time you shoot.</u>

10. <u>Hold the gun perfectly still</u> with absolutely no movement, and then call for the bird.

11. <u>See the bird clearly above the barrel,</u> no flash, and lock on to it with your eyes. Then and only then do you begin your movement to the bird.

12. <u>Move the gun to the bird smoothly and quickly</u> and pass the bead through the bird. And just as the bead is going through the bird, pull/release the trigger. <u>Never stop the gun!</u>

If everything has been done properly, the bird will explode and you will be ready to attack the next bird! Relax and get ready for the next bird.... Isn't this fun!... Enjoy our wonderful sport!

ABOUT THE AUTHOR

The author was born in 1934 in rural Westmoreland County Pennsylvania. He grew up hunting and fishing in the area with his father. Small game hunting was a major family activity at that time.

At age 19 he entered Waynesburg College and graduated with a BS degree in Physics. He then entered the University of Pittsburgh and graduated in 1960 with an MS degree in Nuclear Physics. He taught Physics at Waynesburg College for several years.

After that time he joined Westinghouse Electric Corporation and held many management and technical positions, retiring in 1992.

In 1965 he formed the Imperial Horseshoe Company that manufactured professional pitching horseshoes. Many world and state championships were won using his Imperial horseshoe, and it is still being manufactured.... Horseshoe pitching was an early addiction and was a large part of his life. In 1970, 1973, and 1985 he won the Pennsylvania State Horseshoe Pitching Championship and in 1971 was ranked fifth in the nation.

In 1991 at the age of 57 he discovered the sport of trapshooting. Until that time he had never seen anyone shoot a clay bird. His life has never been the same since! He became addicted almost instantly.

In 1992 he won the High Overall in the local West Penn Trapshooting Club tournament and has been going strong ever since! He won the Senior Veteran Singles Pennsylvania State Championship in 2005 and the Senior Veteran Handicap Pennsylvania State Championship in 2012. Over the years he has won numerous state, local, and regional championships.... His most prestigious win was the Senior Veteran Singles Champion of Champions at the Grand American in Vandalia, OH in 2005.

PUTTING IT ALL TOGETHER

Made in the USA
San Bernardino, CA
02 May 2014